Sara A. Francis Underwood

In love with love:

Four life-studies

Sara A. Francis Underwood

In love with love:
Four life-studies

ISBN/EAN: 9783337871888

Printed in Europe, USA, Canada, Australia, Japan

Cover: Foto ©Andreas Hilbeck / pixelio.de

More available books at **www.hansebooks.com**

In Love with Love

FOUR LIFE-STUDIES

BY

JAMES H. WEST,

Author of "The Complete Life," "Uplifts of Heart and Will,"
"Visions of Good," "Poems," etc., etc.

"*Because I am in love with Love,
And the sole thing I hate is Hate.*"
— Longfellow.

"*I count life just a stuff
To try the soul's strength on.*"
— Browning.

BOSTON
JAMES H. WEST, 174 HIGH STREET
1894

COPYRIGHT, 1894,
BY JAMES H. WEST.

CONTENTS.

	PAGE
TRANSFIGURATIONS,	9
SERENITY,	33
TRUE GREATNESS,	59
OUR OTHER SELVES,	87

I DREAMED the statue of a god
Stood high in every market-place,
That all who thither toiling trod
Might see the beauty of a face
Noble, and freed in every trace
From want, from selfishness, from sin.
Yet seemed it of the human race,
Nor wholly difficult to win.

Indeed, thrice daily, morn, noon, night,
To all the hurriers to and fro
Each statue spake: "The Cosmos bright,
Each gracious force, above, below,
Earth's possibilities but show!
Man can attain whate'er he feels;
Up to the heights 'tis yours to go;
Your gods are but your high ideals."

Is this the Vision of the Race?
This its high nobleness of heart?
Be ours to win that finer grace,
Ours to do valiantly our part!
Thus from the race's ranks shall start
The sonship truly of the Best,
And LOVE's divine and perfect art
Henceforth be man's redeeming quest.

TRANSFIGURATIONS.

'Tis well, O heart, no life of ease
  Before thee opens fair!
That perfect life would fail to please
  Which breathed but softer air.

'Tis not when zephyrs kindly blow,
  And calmly, sweetly steal;
When waters musically flow,
  And laugh along the keel;—

'Tis in the dashing of life's wave,
  And in the sudden shock;
'Tis when the soul, though stout and brave,
  Is ground as on the rock,

That life's objective port is neared,
  Its noblest courses run,
And souls of men the straightest steered
  To Isles of inward Sun.

TRANSFIGURATIONS.

Transfigurations! These are many in human life, or may be many, both in number and in kind. I will speak first of what may be called visible, or physical, transfigurations,—transfigurations, that is to say, of body. Afterwards I will treat of character-transfigurations, — transfigurations, that is, moral, mental and spiritual in men's experience. And finally, in a word or two, of the transfiguration of the race — the exaltation of humanity.

Of visible, bodily transfigurations we certainly all have known. They are frequent. And there is oftentimes great joy in observing them.

Some relative or friend, it may be, has been upon a bed of pain, until the wasting away has been all but complete. Cheeks are sunken, limbs emaciated, color long since gone utterly. But the tide of illness turns, and health begins. Every day, now, there is gain; — in the force of the life-currents that speed through the arteries and veins, in the rounding out of face and limbs once more, in the depth of the hue of health upon the cheeks. And how beautiful and satisfying it all is! It is like the joy and beauty of the Springtime, after the bareness and sadness of winter fields.

And if the transfiguration has not been thus; if the tide of illness has not been turned, but has swept on ruthlessly, until the "transfiguration" has been that solemn and mysterious transfiguration which in our ignorance we call "death," how beautiful and joyful that also! The sleep as of pure marble; the transfiguration of the Angel of the Dawn — the transfiguration into rest and peace. For all is fair and good, and life and death forevermore are one to the preserving power which in its bosom holds and shelters all.

Or, father, mother, let me ask, What has happened to your boy, your girl? — he or she who was your "baby" only a month or two ago. You turn some day to look for your boy. You do not find him. You see in his place a young man. And your girl has become a young woman. The childish plays, the treble voices, are gone; the deepening tones of the boy, which have come with development of chest and with strength of bone and muscle, startle you backward of a sudden, to a period twenty or twenty-five years before, when you yourself were as he — on the boundary-line of manhood, and looking over! Or your girl, mother, carries you back suddenly, as with the wave of a magic wand, to the hour when first you dreamed that "life is Beauty," — yet woke full soon to know that, if indeed Beauty, it is Duty also, and Duty first, in order that the true Beauty may be.

Yet, with all your hopes and fears and anxieties as to what now so speedily must befall the child, whether boy or girl, with what eye of parental pride and satisfaction you behold the mysterious, the mighty "transfiguration" which has come about. And perhaps, as you observe it and wonder over it, rejoicing, farther back yet fly your thoughts,— many times twenty years,— to the words of the writer who, in another hemisphere and civilization altogether from yours, yet with what appropriateness now also, wrote of a certain growing Galilean lad that continually he "increased in wisdom and stature, and in favor with God and man"; and you hope *your* boy may grow to be, in steadfastness of character, such a man as that lad grew to be. The might of the "transfiguration" which now delights your eye will not then have been in vain, and meaningless.

Or, again, there is the slow transfiguration which often comes about in the body of a man or woman who, after years of "animalism" (as we only can call it),— of dissipation or mere brute living; of sensual gratifications and simple pandering to appetites,— strives to throw all this off, and to stand up once more, towards the last, in the true guise of true humanity. No one ever yet quit a hurtful physical habit, of whatever nature, or took up lines of thought-growth and soul-growth, that the body, at once, as well as the mind, did not spring forward to enjoy the new birth and come into its share of the blessing.

"For soul is form, and doth the body make."

And there is no nobler bodily transfiguration than just this, in all the numerous round. For it means struggle, and victory. And such transfiguration, moreover, is holy; for it is the transfiguration of swine's flesh (or no better than that) to the high dignity of a temple for the Holy Spirit of Life,— the evolving and upholding Presence of all worlds.

Then, once more, who has not seen and known the transfigurations which Love often brings about in the human body? And not in isolated and exceptional instances only; nay, but whenever and wherever one shall be "in love with Love."

For one example, what is it that we always mean when we say, of a woman, looking into her face scored and seamed with the life-lines of sympathy and tenderness, "She has the 'mother-look'"? — than which, of a woman, nothing more blessed or joyful could *be* said. Hail indeed, "thou that art highly favored"! the overbrooding Spirit of the Cosmos is with thee! "blessed art thou among women" forever more.

Happy, it is true, are those, unmarried and childless, whose affections and daily living works are set for the good of all around them. Without the comfort, and help, and divine guiding presence of many such, what would this world be? But more blessed, must we not say, the mother! about whose neck infant arms have been flung to the prattle of sweet child-words, and on whose knee in after years the hopeful or weary head of son or daughter, or the brow "flushed, triumphant," has been laid in the confidence and gratitude than which no experience of the human soul is more satisfying or helpful. Such is the benediction of the Highest! The transfiguration of love is the transfiguration of God. Wherever love is, God is. We live in the upholding energy, and it in us.

And the bodily transfiguration which comes of love is by no means monopolized by parents. There is the bodily transfiguration — the physical illumination, through love — of those whom well and often we call the world-saviours.

One day, many hundred years ago, when Gautama Buddha, the Truth Revealer of India, was first looking out upon the world with eye of love, longing to bring it into peace, he met certain experiences of woe and death in his fellow-mortals which touched his soul, always sympathetic, with even more than ordinary power.

"And lo! he turned
Eyes gleaming with divine tears to the sky,
Eyes lit with heavenly pity to the earth;

From sky to earth he looked, from earth to sky,
As if his vision sought in lonely flight
Some far-off vision, linking this and that,
Lost,— past,— but searchable, and seen, and known.
Then cried he, while his lifted countenance
Glowed with the burning passion of a love
Boundless, insatiate: 'Let all the sins
That ever were committed in this world
Descend on me, that all the world may be
Delivered.'". . .

That all the world might be delivered! What love and desire indeed was that! great as the love and desire of a God — of a God "in the highest." What wonder that, in the eyes of all those who — unknown to him — were observers of this his love and cross and passion, he seemed, as he stood uttering his divine cry, to be "transfigured" in face and form, a halo of glory gleaming about his head; divine light flashing even from his garments?

There is a transfiguration, similar to this of the Buddha's, recorded in the life of another of the world-saviours. Jesus of Galilee had been speaking to his disciples, and to the waiting multitude around about, of "bearing one another's burdens";—of thus helping to decrease the world's woe and want and sin. This was a frequent, indeed this was almost the only topic, with Jesus. His own sensitive soul, like the soul of Gautama five centuries before, was "touched with the feeling," godlike, divine, for human "infirmities" and human needs; and he too,—again like Gautama,—longed that the "chastisement" of the world's peace might be upon him.

Speaking after this manner, therefore, to his disciples, on the occasion which we have in mind, he then, in one of his finest aphorisms, summed up the consequences, in this life, both of selfishness and of generosity. "Whosoever will 'save' his life," he said,—that is, use it only for himself, for his own selfish ends,—"shall as good as lose it; for it will not amount to very much. But whosoever gladly will 'lose' his life (as the world estimates selflessness) for the sake of man, shall find it again, and more than find it — in the divine inward blessedness that comes to him." And then, taking Peter and James, and John his brother, he brought them up "into a high mountain apart." And while they walked and talked with him, — he still discoursing to them on his favorite theme, the theme of the divineness of human selflessness and of struggle for man's uplifting, — behold, he "was transfigured before them, and his face did shine as the sun, and his raiment was white as the light."

Again a transfiguration of love was this! — of the world-love radiant in Jesus' own soul, flashing even, as it seemed, from his face and clothing; and of the answering love, the sympathy and awakened high desire, of those who heard him.

Would any man, would any woman, in body and face grow beautiful? Be their souls filled with love for Truth and Man!

There are transfigurations of the body that are transfigurations of martyrdom. A swift example of these is brought to mind through its connection with the last. Jesus now is gone. He has met, and met bravely, the fate ever in reserve for the outspoken "radical" in matters of religious belief, and lies in the tomb hewn out in the rock;—"wherein no man"? nay! wherein many men, both before him and since, have lain. But some few, out of the hundreds who had heard his words,—the few who had caught a flash at least, now and then, of his real meaning,— were laboring to propagate his truth, even though he himself had been taken away. And persecution meets them likewise. One of them, as a warning to the rest, is taken out by the mob,— Stephen, his name was. And in the public streets he is stoned to death. But those "looking steadfastly on him,"— knowing why he died, and entering, many of them, even against their will, into something of his own enthusiasm for man,—"saw his face," though streaming with blood, as lately they had seen it also in the council-hall, "as it had been the face of an angel." Dying for man he was irradiated by the divine, the God.

An example similar to that of Stephen comes to us in a picture by Millais. It is of a woman standing on English shores, knee deep in the rising tide. She is bound to a stake, and the slowly incoming waters surge and swell around her. There are men and women on the beach, but there is no hope for her. She has been doomed, by certain.pious judges, to die, and this is the manner of her execution. There is no terror however, no sadness even, in her look. Her eyes are turned upward, and from them seems to stream a great light. Again it is the light of love! — of willing sacrifice for a great end. Below the picture are printed certain lines, the idea in which has been transcribed thus:

> "Murdered, for owning Truth supreme!
> Murdered for this and no more crime!
> Within the sea tied to a stake
> She died for Faith's and Virtue's sake."

By the hand of Religion she died for the sake of religion! What anomaly here! And she died drowned in the pitiless waters, yet transfigured in light!— what fact a million times repeated in the world's history! while her soul sped to blessedness on the wings of love for her kind, and of desire that all men might see the Good and be saved.

Bodily transfigurations are many. We have recounted a few of them.

There are also the commoner, the daily transfigurations in human lives, meeting the observation of all; transfigurations in ways of *character*,— for good or evil,— no less valuable for consideration.

In the past, as all the world now knows, man has been wonderfully transfigured,— from the brutish coming into the human, from weakness coming into strength, from meanness into power. Before humanity now, lies the task of progressing infinitely onward from these. From the simply human, man must go on and up to the divine! From simple strength and ingenuity he must go onward and upward to soul-beauty, to spiritual perfection. He can! Then he must. And he shall; for it is the law of Nature. It is the order of the universe.

> "Every clod feels a stir of might,
> An instinct within it that reaches and towers,
> And, groping blindly above it for light,
> Climbs to a soul in grass and flowers."

Exactly so with man. The divine Power which in the far ages back evolved the "grasses and flowers," dwelling within them,— speaking to the Midian shepherd in the bush of roses, speaking to Jesus in the lilies of the field; the divine Power which from the nebulous haze evolved the chaotic cell-masses, and from the chaotic cell-masses the climbing life of the world through the whole ascending series, plant, animal and man,— is still surging and swelling, within the soul of all that we call human; and still shall, we feel, strive with man, and unceasingly, till he comes, far off, into his perfect birthright — his birthright of that Ideal, that Noble, that Holy, that Blessed Best, which in all ages of conscious life has thrilled in man's brain and soul in prophecy, singing Vedas and Psalms and Sagas of coming Good.

Character transfigurations? There is always growth, transfiguration of soul, increase of manly strength and power, in so simple a thing even as the stout bearing of life's daily burdens, — regardless of what the burdens may be. How often we sink under them, instead of bravely bearing them up! Come! we must hide our hurts; — we must not always show them. There is strength in pain-bearing; in overcoming odds. The truth is, we are not very courageous, the most of us. We shrink from hard things. We ought to be glad of them! — glad that they come to us, so that we can use them and build ourselves up through them. "I count life just a stuff to try the soul's strength on and educe the man"! Why be always over-sensitive to the thousand ills of life? — above all, to the innumerable little, miserable spites and meannesses all about us, irritating, even exasperating though they indeed seem at times? Banish them from the thought. Ten-fold, be we ourselves never guilty of such. Be we nobler. And in the greater things be we heroic. Then neither illness nor poverty, nor the treachery of those we counted our friends, nor any evil whatever, shall harm us. Let us "transfigure" all these. We may. And in their transfiguration, into good, we shall find *ourselves* becoming transfigured — into sweetness and serenity and humility. All life's sad things, bad things, may become for us,— in the poet's phrase,— if we master them, if we use them aright, even as

"Jewels five words long,
That on the stretch'd forefinger of all Time
Sparkle forever."

And there are transfigurations more directly of spiritual growth, through *mental* growth.

We need, how much, every day, for our comfort in sorrow, for our aid in perplexity, for our rest in weariness, for our companionship in loneliness, for our peace in life-disappointments, all the "transfiguration" of soul which can possibly and in any way come to us, from communion either with the Infinite Spirit of Nature or with the sages and seers of all past and the present time. And the Spirit here fails us not, ever,— if we but know how to woo it and to be wooed by it! We seek ever, we say,—with slow and painful steps,— the eternal life; and we know not well where to look: we go wandering. "Build new domes of Thought in your mind," one says to us, "and presently you will find that, instead of your finding the eternal life, the eternal life has found you." True forever.

Do we think we lack the "leisure" for study and thought? A half hour a day is eighteen days of ten hours each a year! Beyond this is at least the Sunday afternoon and evening of each week,— an endless succession of Sunday afternoons and evenings. What opportunity indeed for "excursions"! — into noble fields of science, of poetry, of the higher fiction. What journeys may be made, at one's own fireside, into foreign lands,— seeing perhaps with others' eyes better than one ever could with one's own. What hours of blessedness one may spend with those who shall tell of the might and marvel of the human soul.

> "I am owner of the sphere,
> Of the seven stars and the solar year,
> Of Cæsar's hand, and Plato's brain,
> Of Lord Christ's heart, and Shakspere's strain."

All these are mine — and thine. Or *may* be. Then, friend, through your coming days and years, let not Sunday after Sunday and night after night of mere frivolous reading, or mere pastime, of wasted high opportunities, mar and hold back your progress *as a soul* through possible countless eons yet to be! Have some hard task always on hand, whether of book or deed.

Some *hard* task. On the heights only is or ever shall be blessedness. Immortality shall be meaningless to the unfit. If you are ever to reach the heights you must climb. If, mentally and spiritually, you are indeed ever to be "transfigured" you must sometime begin. Why not now?

And there are moral transfigurations.

Do any of us ever feel that we are not in need morally? Look deep within! "Every thought of unkindness, every unfair, hard judgment, every trembling regard of the outward or bold disregard of the inward life, is a siding with the spirit of evil against the spirit of good." What shall we say, then, of the grosser, the often hideous faults, of which many of us know that we are possessed? In the eye of the Ideal where do we stand?

How many low things, things of evil, things of unfairness, things down-dragging, there are about us in the world, which in the painting of our life-pictures we copy! We are asked what we would think of an artist of fine powers who should paint only old rusty pots and battered tin cans and ragged cloths, and faded bouquets disported in cracked vases? Yet there are myriads of men who seem to fashion their lives only after things like to these; while the whole world of beauty — of lake and river, tree and flower, mountain and meadow, of delightful literature, and of high, divine human faces and souls — lies open to their skill.

Is the reminder needless which comes to us, that many an otherwise noble man has been dragged down from a splendid possible career by some one evil habit, some one unholy passion, some one ungoverned appetite, — just as you saw that that fine tree which you met a week or a month ago in your Sunday afternoon ramble with God in the woods or by the pond-side had been slowly killed by one contemptible, poisonous, clinging vine? And many more of us, in lesser ways, really drive out all or much of the possible joy and hope and blessedness of our lives by the retention of some one single miserable small failing — of impatience, or harsh criticism, or tale-bearing, or unfair dealing, or love of show and pretence, or some base, evil passion. But all of this, small as well as great, must go, and we must work to that end; or — never the "transfiguration" for us! Only aggravation and heart-sickness and ignes-fatui forever more!

Happy we, if, each new day, transfigurations of some high nature are present — always in process — in our souls; as they are eternally present in outward Nature and in the life of the race.

There remains a closing word.

To make our transfiguration complete, to make it divine, it must be of ourselves not only; others must be partakers with us of our blessedness.

Not for ourselves only, the comfort and the joy! Not for us alone, the roominess of home, the uplifting of books, the fresh air of country ways, the divine insight of souls. In larger measure and by far wiser means than now in vogue by any church or political party or "charity" organization over the world, the good of all — the *real* good of all — must be sought, and by all, that the real transfiguration of the race, of mankind as a whole, may ever actually, in its fulness, come to pass, and the kingdoms of this world become in truth, as the world so long has prayed, the kingdom of Good and of God. There is no transfiguration in selfishness. Be our hearts turned also outward to the world. Be we in love with love!

"Heaven's gate is shut to him who comes alone:
Save thou a soul, and it shall save thine own."

SERENITY.

ALL day my maples in the blast have bowed;
　The sleet howls lustily through shivering limbs;
　Yet e'en though ice the creaking branches rims,
Here from my window watch I him so proud —
Dear feathered preacher! Full and sweet and loud
　His warbling cheer the wintry whistling dims.
　So amid persecution rose the hymns
Of dearest trust from Christians newly vowed.

Soul of my soul! for secret, sheltered nook
　Must thou forever pray when blasts are nigh
　And howling passions, seeking thee, stream by?
Nay, O my soul, in the gale's teeth dare look!
　Still fighting, sing! lift undismayed thy din:
　Only undaunted hearts scale heaven and win.

SERENITY.

It is a commonplace that people of different age, of different temperament and position in life, look upon the world and on human existence with largely different eye. The boy of fourteen or sixteen years, whose whole soul is bound up in base-ball, in boating and bathing and horseback-riding; whose supper is always ready for him at fifteen minutes past six o'clock, and whose digestion is as unconscious for him as the circulation of his blood, finds little to complain of in the world. The young fellow of eighteen or twenty, who has never worked a day in his life except for fun; whose every want has been gratified; for whom suns have risen in glory and set in peace; for whom airs have blown only to fan his brow or waft his sail, thinks the world a pretty good world. The young miss of sixteen, who (while her mother or the house-maid bakes the bread and sweeps the rooms) chases polkas and mazurkas pitilessly back and forth over a key-board; who has known a school-girl love or two, and been to the Opera House occasionally to see Mary Anderson or some other as Juliet, dreams life happy and romantic.

Look on this picture — and on this! There are myriads on myriads for whom existence is a very different thing indeed from what has been hinted at; for whom the work and weariness and hungers of life open early and continue long. There are boys of fifteen, or young girls of the same age, on whom, by the death of father or mother, the care of a family of little, eager, feverish hearts has suddenly fallen. There are mothers left early widows, painfully anxious for their children's future. There are shop-girls by thousands, wearily working for a few dollars a week to keep life

within and clothing upon them. There are
strong, skilled men, able and willing to work
and work hard, yet bound down to meager
wages by the prevalent harmful systems of
greed and competition in business. There are
earnest young souls filled with conscious
possibilities of noble action and high attainment, yet who are restricted sharply, by
circumstances, to the common round, the
trivial task. There are mothers weeping for
little-ones snatched away by early death; wives
and children despairing under the dissipations or
tyranny of thoughtless or passionate husbands
and fathers; mothers mourning over wayward
sons. There are social and religious reformers,
weary with the apathy of those who might do
better,— rebuffed by the heartlessness or care-
lessness of those who might encourage and
assist.

And the list is by no means yet full. There
are hundreds of thousands of others, all over
the world,— in hovel and in palace, in senates

and in shops, in factory and in parlor,— bound down and worn out, and forever exasperated, by the thousand and ten thousand other smaller or larger patience-trying events and accidents common to human life: hereditary disease, invalid friends, dishonest neighbors, careless helpers or workmen, the breath of public slander, contaminating local politics, the petty disagreeablenesses of relatives, the loss of money, unprofitable business,— thousands of things. And for all these people,— whatever their grievance, large or small,— the world, if it ever ran smoothly for them (which they doubt), seems now to have jumped a cog somewhere, and to continue persistently to spin upside down.

"All miserable enough," we say,—"and all inexplicable!" But is it inexplicable?

Moreover, life's *little* hardnesses and harassments often worry us as much, and are as difficult to bear, as its severer trials; tax our patience more, perhaps. And, as a whole, we fret and fret, and rub against mental and spiritual briars, till our faces are thin with mourning, and our hearts thinner.

Serenity! Serenity!—where does it abide? Serenity! it is this which I urge. Notwithstanding everything,— serenity!

Yet I would not be misunderstood. Not serenity under any trial or grief or injustice which ought to be righted and which might be righted! The world is full of such, and is religiously slothful over them — "piously" patient, culpably serene over them. Not of such, but of things which *cannot* be helped, I speak. Not under inertia and shiftlessness, serenity. But under everything done that can be done; under everything done as well and as faithfully as, under present conditions, it may be done,— serenity! Yes, even though injustice does still, in some part, reign,— if we are actually doing all we can to right it; even though sickness and loss and want, and misunderstandings, and miseries larger or less, do continue about us, wrapping us around and around,— if we are not culpable in any way regarding them, but are earnest always, and hopeful,— serenity, I say!

And doubtless even in the greater disasters of life occasion for righteous calmness of soul, such as that of which I am speaking, comes much oftener than many are disposed to believe. For every man who is filled full, as those to-day of the forward look are, with the world's newer ethical and religious thought, which does completely away with all old wildernesses of implicit belief in infinite arbitrariness; the thought and faith which are almost petulantly impatient of the hindrances and childishnesses which men still accept as eternal verities,— for every earnest man to-day there is, in this newer thought, the possibility of Peace such as the world never before knew. We dwell in a universe of order and brightness. Through co-operation with the forces of good all desirable attainment is freely open to us. We are brought to real grief only through ignorance or wilfulness. We lose much then, unnecessarily, out of our lives, in giving way, ever, under even great trials; and particularly through our ethical fretfulnesses and our religious impatiences. How much more do we lose, then, through *irreligious* lack of calm — our turbulence and surf-beating in commoner things.

Too much, surely, we cannot be bound up in the great needs of man; in thought and work for the elevation of "society at large." So much is there, in the world, of injustice and oppression; so much of browbeating and heartlessness; so much of poverty and passion and conceit and ignorance making these others possible, that over-exertion on our part in behalf of "the Calamity" (as Carlyle and Emerson were wont sometimes to call earth's evil and degraded classes) is impossible. On the contrary, we feel we cannot do one tithe of what we would. We rejoice in the creation

of all new public-parks and the building of all
"sanitary tenement-houses"; in all regenerative
institutions like Toynbee Hall in London and
the Hull House in Chicago, and the upbuilding,
redemptive work of Felix Adler in New York
city. We are glad of all Sunday openings of
libraries and art-galleries; of all free night
schools and systems of industrial education;
of the marvelously growing prominence given
to-day by the press and platform to all phases
of problems bearing on labor and other social
reforms. We rejoice in all evidences of a
growing power in the labor-ranks themselves,
so far as that power is wisely, not foolishly,
manifested. Even the wilder, more determined
demonstrations of workless throngs are not
without their decisive value, we deem, as city
streets, both in America and Europe, are
oftener and oftener filled now by multitudes
clamoring for larger possibilities. All these
things mean the education of public sentiment.
And it is educated public sentiment, alone,

that ever brings about any species of great practical, permanent reform. The people must be able to bear the advance before the advance can really come in its highest good.

For this reason there is satisfaction in noting all the things I have named; and we are continually urging ourselves on to work heartily in all possible ways, with voice and pen, brain and hand, to hasten even more the coming time of good,— the day earth's prophets long have sought. This, moreover, not only in the matter of labor reform, but of marriage and temperance also, and of all species of human uplifting; in the matter, too, of the purification and sublimation of religion from its many still-perpetuated follies.

Yet what multitudes of men and women there are to-day — they are numbered among the best and the noblest — who are not *serene* in all this high work and hope! who are over-turbulent, or at any rate unnecessarily fretful and anxious in the mighty task. Doing, indeed, perhaps, everything actually possible under present conditions; helping on in the progress all we can, our blood nevertheless, at certain times of unusual excitement, surges to the boiling point and continues there for hours; the muscles of our limbs twitch nervously; our brains seem on fire; our lips send out hot torrents of words. In five minutes we waste a day's, or possibly a week's vitality; take it right out of our bodies and souls. So also in many moments of commoner and often really insignificant excitement, over events in shop or house or street even. Take it right out of our bodies and souls, I say; — and that is just it! That is why I deprecate the disquietudes into which we permit ourselves to fall; why I call for serenity. The wise man is economical of his nervous dissipations. We and the world need every grain of energy, every last item of vitality, possible for us to hoard up. *We* need it, in our bodies and souls; and the world, to-day, in its progressive life.

Do you imagine that Garrison and Phillips could ever have done their mighty work, facing for years the passionate, aristocratic mobs that howled in their faces, if they had worn themselves all out, persistently, with excitement and turbulence, or with over-impatience? No; they were content to work,— however in one sense passionately,— yet "on long lines." And serenity was theirs! Garrison kept the type clicking in his composing-stick, at work on his *Liberator*, even while the mob, club-armed, was howling at his printing-office door. And on another occasion, when the rope had just been around his neck, he was the coolest man in the demoniac-streets.

With a wave of his hand, and the calm front of his serene presence, Phillips quelled the frequent devil in his audiences — exorcised the fiend, and sent it headlong down a steep place into the sea, while the freed souls of his listeners stayed to be thrilled through and through with the persuasive accents of his tongue.

Do you imagine that Parker and Emerson could have done their great work if they had turned to "mouth back" at every one of the carping religionists who banned them, or if they had fretted and fumed inwardly at every word of reproach; if they had struck sparks in their hearts at every unmerited condemnation? No; Parker was serene, and great. And as for Emerson,—" Good-by, proud world," he sang, with heroic cheerfulness; "I'm going to my own hearth-stone, bosomed in the green hills alone." Thou art not my friend, O world,—but what of that? I am thine!

> "Good-by, to Flattery's fawning face;
> To Grandeur with his wise grimace;
> To upstart Wealth's averted eye;
> To supple Office low and high;
> To crowded halls, to court and street;
> To frozen hearts and hasting feet.
>
> "Oh, when I am safe in my sylvan home,
> I tread on the pride of Greece and Rome;
> And when I am stretched beneath the pines,
> Where the evening star so holy shines,

> I laugh at the pride and the lore of man,
> At the sophist schools and the learnèd clan:
> For what are they all, in their high conceit,
> When man in the bush with God may meet?"

Or read that stirring poem-hymn by Mrs. Sara A. Underwood:

> "Swift-beating Heart, in patience curb
>   Thy eager throbs, thy wild desire!
> Nor let opposing foes disturb
>   Thy aim, nor quench thy steadfast fire.
>
> "Patience, stern Will! Though sluggish moves
>   The high event thou would'st control,
> Forget not, wheels that form new grooves
>   In virgin soil are hard to roll.
>
> "Patience, bold Brain! the startled crowd,
>   Who 'think in herds,' ne'er yet did greet
> New truth with acclamations loud,
>   Until crowned victor o'er defeat.
>
> "Patience, brave Toiler! Duty asks
>   Thy isolation. Fear not thou!
> In loneliness the grandest tasks
>   Were ever wrought, and shall be now!"

Let those of us who are impatient and over-anxious at the world's slow progress, take this word of strength and serenity into our hearts, and live by it; permit it to "quiet" us.

A suggestion of serenity in certain departments of life and thought more directly personal comes to us. I refer to the often disappointing field of our *intellectual* life; to the perplexities and losses of business, and to the matter of our direct private, hopeful interest in public politics. In all these, how frequently, after being as faithful as we may, our grief and disappointment, on account of marked lack of progress in the things dear to us, overcome our discretion, and again we fret and chafe till life is dreary to us.

What if we cannot read and study all we would like to? Do we do what we can? Oftentimes it doesn't need more than one high thought — some single radiant phrase from Carlyle or Ruskin, some scintillant verse from Goethe or Clough — to make a whole day blessed for us, if only we seize on it in the morning, or perchance over night just as we fall asleep. Its helpfulness and high enchantment follow us in our dreams, and through all our waking hours near by. Serenity is thine and mine!

In business, what if the dollars are a few less, at the end of the year, than we expected, provided we have enough of what is due us to square us with the world? It is often, we well may feel, only because our wants are over many, that we are in such frequent pitiable plight. We persistently forget, if we ever heard, what the rudely-strong peasant-hero of Craigenputtock suggested to us years ago: "The Fractional Blessedness of Life can be increased in value not so much by increasing your Numerator as by lessening your Denominator."

Why do we want so many things! Are they absolutely necessary? Oh, one look at the stars! Oh, one trill of a bird! Oh, the first spring hepatica! Oh, the clasp of a little child's arms! And *with* these, the thoughts that do often lie too deep for tears! How much better a little, including these,— a little, with divine serenity,— than an overplus of life's mere upholsteries with eternal discontent,— the clouds never off the soul!

And in the matter of our interest in affairs national,— though here indeed there seems a real offense and stumbling-block ever present with us,— can we do as much good, help matters along as fast, by tearing a passion to tatters; declaring purity and honesty dead in the world; as by a calm, cool, serene view of things, and a long-headed persistence in personal well-doing, with a constant cry in the wilderness? The shame to a thousand American communities, however, is not so much that they often lack serenity in their view of widest public affairs, as that in their own little local politics there are men often caring more for gratifying a petty spite, or showing a personal grudge, than for the election of clean, pure officials.

Even here, however,— serenity! We know

the good age will come; for city and for continent it will come,— far off,— if we all help it on a little. Patience then, and serenity, I say,— till we

> "See the golden beam incline
> To the side of perfect justice, mastered by a faith divine."

If men really are not faithful locally, however, they will never be faithful nationally. And if weak in the minor things of social duty they well may be "pestered," forever, with even Dantean discomfitures. Political — like spiritual — serenity will never meet us more than half way.

And still another range of thought and feeling of close personal import our topic may include. There is serenity in the matter of our more direct personal grievances and downbearings — our *family* aches and sorrows.

Looking out over the small circle even of our own knowledge, whose heart, if at all sensitive, is not at times low-bowed, in view of the frequent tragedies and mockeries of what is called, by the world, "home." Glorious opportunity here, for many, for the beauty born of heroic sorrow! Balzac's fine word recurs to us. Balzac's word is *Strength.*

Surely, however, we hardly need the suggestion that it should be a part of the "religion" of all men and women bravely and divinely to "bear up" under their private miseries. Yet this should be a practical and "saving" religion, since in the very act of thus "bearing," if done with high, unselfish, thoughtful, purposeful intent, the loftiest heights of human peace, of human greatness, yes, of human-divine blessedness, become ours. The power to suffer and to *endure,*— at the same time growing thereby,— this is the measure of the spirit's heights and depths. Even amid direst woes, serenity of soul! — it is the poet's dream, the prophet's vision, the wise man's and wise woman's eternal endeavor.

Be *thou* strong!

"There is no light in earth or heaven
  But the cold light of stars;
And the first watch of night is given
  To the red planet Mars.

"O star of Strength! I see thee stand
  And smile upon my pain;
Thou beckonest with thy mailèd hand
  And I am strong again.

"The star of the unconquered Will,
  He rises in my breast,
Serene, and resolute, and still,
  And calm, and self-possessed.

"O fear not in a world like this,
  And thou shalt know, ere long,
Know how sublime a thing it is
  To suffer — and be strong."

A simple call to serenity amid the stir, the pain, the discouragement often in the hearts of men and women in times of their own personal, private struggle with temptation, or other direct evil influence of passion, may fitly be presented.

I do not understand, as I endeavor to read the human soul, guessing something at its origin, that to fail sometimes is blackness of darkness,— however high may be my Moral

Ideal, nor how terrible wilfulness in sin may
seem to me. Are we in love with love? — that
is the main thing! We are not yet angels;
we are men and women,— or slowly becoming
men and women, rising up from something
lower to something higher. When we become
wholly angelic,— that is to say, altogether
perfect,— the time will have come for us to
go elsewhere. This world is not a world of
perfection, and would be no place for a prodigy
of the Adam kind. It is a world for *growth* —
and for growth often through failure. May
we not count it a true word, "We must
not expect unbroken progress as yet, in
every department of a life imperfect through
its very nature"? All that we can do is to
struggle to the very best of our ability —
though who, in reality, even rarely, does as
much as that! All that we *can* do is to
hate the evil with a perfect hatred, recognizing
it as moral death, struggling heroically, deter-
minedly, against it; being in love with love,

and forever striving towards it; and then let serenity come in and bless us.

Why go mourning all our days? Let us look up and not down, forward and not back. I honestly believe that the great majority of earnest men and women want to do the best they can. They need encouragement, not fault-finding.

I am not saying (I perhaps should make more prominently manifest) that wilful evil is not a deplorable thing. I would leave no possible loophole for selfish excuse. Transgression is a deplorable thing, always. It degrades a soul!—holds it back upon its upward way. But to dwell on "failure"— to seem to believe only in failure—is not good. The rather, to let the serenity of the universe's own eternal Peace come in to us and bless us,—as it will, if we will receive it, —that is good. And simply to struggle even, earnestly, against temptation, and to feel that thus we are fighting old Chaos,— fighting darkness, and freeing the light,— is, in itself, the index-road to serenity; while as for that deeper *after*-serenity which comes *from* struggle, it is "the life of God" in *our* life, as Matthew Arnold sings to us. It is the divine part of the universe dwelling in us, abiding with us.

The capacity for moral suffering is that which really makes us men; is that which leads into blessedness. A man who has no moral sensitiveness,— he is not a man: he is yet in Nature's brute-stage. That which made Jesus great, that which made Channing great, that which makes all great ones great, is sensitiveness to moral and social shortcomings, sensitiveness to injustice, sensitiveness to sin. But Jesus and Channing were serene also — divinely serene. And so shall any man be, if he be great. It is only weakness that falters, fumes, is full of jars; while Power and Peace go hand in hand.

"Earth, whirled amid the stars,
Wakes not a nested bird or slumbering child."

If we live truly, Emerson wisely says, we shall see truly. "It is as easy for the strong man to be strong as it is for the weak man to be weak."

And when once we begin to recognize that we — all of us, each one individually, not a few high souls only — are capable of soul-perceptions; capable of thought-flashes and helpfulnesses which are direct gleams in our souls, always, from out of the universal soul, we shall gladly then disburden our lives and memories, at once and permanently, of much early-world phantasy, which, retained, is but hindrance to us, and be thenceforth free, serene, forevermore. When a man comes really to dwell in the divine; to know that the universe is his,— or he, at any rate, a fragment of the universe, a fragment of its Mighty Life, and heir to all,— then shall his voice be "sweet as the murmur of the brook and the rustle of the corn." When a man comes really to dwell thus in the divine,— *living* in love with love,—

his life shall be peace. The pettinesses of life assume their proper place. The lack of "money" will not sicken the soul, even though it inconvenience the body. The slowness of the world to see Truth and to put Justice into being will not distress one over much, nor hinder one's further efforts in the same persistent line. If one voluntarily forego a meal now and then, in order that something better may be his or be another's, the pomegranates of Eden will quiet and fatten his inner, spiritual life, if indeed the lack of milk and bread shall give his stomach a pang. Moral endeavor will be beautiful in his sight. All will be light, not dark; encouraging, not disheartening.

And serenity like this is worth striving for! I will say, too, that if we attain to it,— as we all may attain to it,— goodness and mercy shall follow us all the days of our life. We shall not feel painfully the want of any good thing.

TRUE GREATNESS.

O EARNEST Fathers !   Sweet-faced Sisterhood !
Martyrs and Saints of whate'er faith or dress
Who through the years left no man comfortless ;
In thought of others — self in self subdued —
Striving to make mankind more pure and good ;
Fain by the warning word or breathed caress
To stay earth's evil and perfidiousness ;
Scourged, censured, lacking bread and habitude !

Would that To-day — this trebly fine To-day —
We thy helped brothers 'mid the world's mad strife
Might through thy love and sacrifices rare
Be led to walk thy same strong, towering way :
Calming the world that hungereth for life
By breath of Brotherhood's supernal air.

TRUE GREATNESS.

As in childhood and youth we studied history, and in later years have read more and more in this line, certain prominent historic characters have continually met us,— representatives of all lands and times,— bearing the title of "the Great." Macedonia gave the world Alexander the Great; Russia was first made into a nation by Peter the Great; Prussia, and Europe at large, knew the tyranny and the treachery of Frederick the Great; France was led through turmoil and blood by Napoleon the Great. Many others also have borne the title, whom I need not stay to mention.

What shall we say of those whom I have already named? Were they really great? This depends, of course, altogether upon our standard of greatness. All, without question, were able men, leaders of their fellows. All of them, perhaps, were at times generous, and occasionally self-sacrificing. All of them were inured to hardship,— they accepted this, indeed, as the price of their greatness. And all, undoubtedly, directly or indirectly, were means of the world's advance. But Alexander was a glutton and a drunkard. On the whole, moreover, he was ambitious only for self: no thought of the good of mankind in general ever entered his mind or heart. "He was a robber on a gigantic scale, and justly to be classed with ruffians." He was "great"— in ambitious wickedness.

Peter of Russia was a man of powerful and original genius, a worker with his own hands, and the well-wisher of his people. He was the builder of Russia's prosperity. But he was, at the same time, a man of violent passions and immoral excesses; and a fighter of fierce battles not in the cause of right, but simply for the acquisition of new territory and of power upon the sea. He was "great"— in national avarice.

Frederick of Prussia, who lived a century later, is one of Carlyle's "heroes,"— not, however, because he was pure and noble, unselfish and humanitarian, for he was none of these; but (in Carlyle's own language) "because he managed not to be a liar and a charlatan, as the rest of his century was"; and moreover, because he was a man of mighty will-power. Carlyle thought that the energy and determination of Frederick, if brought to bear on the pure and progressive things of the world, by men devoted to the good and to humanity's advance, would insure as gracious results for the world as Frederick's powers brought a mighty name and fame for himself and his nation. And so they would. But Frederick himself, with all his financial wisdom and ability as a warrior, was at the same time unjust and cruel. If oftentimes he was indeed not "a liar and a charlatan," then these words have no meaning for us: his broken political treaty with Maria Theresa of Austria, alone, would prove this, and the character of his private life points finger of shame along the same road. In the life of Frederick there is little but his energy and his will-power that is commendable.

So we come now to the fourth "great one" whom I named,— Napoleon Bonaparte. And what of him? His life reads like a romance. It is ever new to us. It is dazzling and tremendous. No wonder he was, as Emerson says, the darling of his soldiers — and their dare-devil; the envy of business-men everywhere, for his brilliant power of success; the shining-light of mechanics and literary folk alike, for his superabundance of knowledge and skill in both these directions; "the idol of common men, because he had in transcendent degree the qualities and powers of common men." And yet, at the same time, he was a man utterly lacking in all moral qualities, a high-handed criminal and deceiver, "thoroughly unscrupulous," an "exorbitant egotist," perfidious, vulgar, infamous. In his life was once more demonstrated, in the world's history, the "experiment under the most favorable conditions, of the powers of intellect without conscience. Never was such a leader so endowed, and so weaponed; never leader found such aids and followers. And what was the result of this vast talent and power, of these immense armies, burned cities, squandered treasures, immolated millions of men,— and of this demoralized Europe? It came to no result. All passed away, like the smoke of his artillery, and left no trace. He left France smaller, poorer, feebler, than he found it, and the whole contest for freedom was to be begun again." Napoleon the "Great"!

The thought comes to us perforce, just here, that if we are indeed to attempt a "list" of great men, it shall not be, at all, of kings and warriors! It shall be, the rather, of prophets, poets, scientists, inventors, and the workers in the humbler field of any single human brother's need. These and these only are the world's truly great ones (so far as the truly great can be put into "list" at all). The truly great are those,— men or women,— who have led the world on in love and truth and beauty; who have been its saviours from evil; its pointers to ideals, to progress, to human brotherhood; its revealers of the mystery and might of the universe, and of the heights of divine possibility within the human soul. The world's great men have not been, at all, its conquerors in war, but its promoters of peace. Confucius, and Gautama, and Isaiah, and Socrates and Jesus, and all the long line of hopeful spiritual ones from their day down; Copernicus and Spinoza and Newton and Humboldt and Darwin and Spencer, and their scientific brotherhood; Gutenburg and Stephenson and Morse, and their inventive co-laborers; Shakspere and Goethe and Emerson, and their divine literary compatriots,— all these are the "world-saviours," and these are really great. "He that will be first among you, let him be servant of all."

But it is not any "list" of great men, whether so-called by the world or not; nor, indeed, any "greatness" that can well be listed, of which I wish mainly to speak in this address. It is of the greatness, the *real* greatness, possible in every individual human soul, in very simple ways. In very *simple* ways, I say; yet difficult, too, and sublime, and taxing to the utmost all our courage and patience and skill. And that this is the true statement of the case you will at once agree when I name, as the first of the two high tokens of real greatness concerning which I shall particularly speak, *the divine power of overcoming.* Of overcoming! A power into which we have to grow: not a power often "born" in men, coming without struggle.

I do not suppose that the power to overcome,— whatever the object or evil in mind,— was ever born, in its full glory, in any man. No, not even in the man Jesus himself; though in the mistaken adoration of hundreds of years Jesus has come down to us as one entirely sinless,— morally pure and spiritually unruffled from the very beginning, through supernatural power. It is not necessary to my faith and endeavor to believe that Jesus was always sinless. Indeed, the contrary is true. Certainly he himself never claimed to be sinless. The rather, we know that when about thirty years of age he was, at his own request, baptized by John with the baptism which was of "repentance," and "for the remission of sin." And on another and later occasion, when a would-be questioner came to him, addressing him, "Good Master," Jesus interrupted with, "Why callest thou me good?" Moreover, that Jesus was always "spiritually unruffled" is an idea disproved by more than one direct incident related of him in the Gospels.

But what of all this! — he was a man, a kingly man! a struggler with himself to the last; a wrestler with the evil and the weakness within him, and with the evil and the weakness around him. And later on in his career, when he was approaching his death, he could say to his followers, in the grandest words (to my mind) which he ever uttered, "I indeed, in my lifetime, have met trial, and sorrow, and disappointment, and persecution; I have also known defeat: tears have been my meat day and night. So, in this world, shall you and all others, who strive for the good, meet tribulation likewise. *But be of good cheer, I have overcome the world,* — and so may you."

Yes, at some triumphant time in his life, — even if not till towards the end, — and notwithstanding all the evil and labor and loss and frequent temptation in his past experience, — he could stand up before his fellows, and say, "I have overcome! I, and not the world, am victor; I am ready to depart. Moreover, here is example and encouragement for you. Follow me,— follow in my road,— and ye shall be saved also!" His noblest words of all!

And we all indeed must follow. For we all have our evil things, our shames and weaknesses, to overcome; and if we too, like Jesus and all other great ones in the world, are to stand up, even at the last, in conscious power and freedom, all the evil in us must *be* overcome. And here indeed shall be greatness.

This much concerning the evil and shame and weakness in us,— the pettiness and frivolity, the avarice and the vanity and the passion. There are also other qualities, or tendencies, of a somewhat different kind, in our nature, concerning which we have to be perpetually on guard. There are many evils and lackings of a social and business kind which it is no less our duty to overcome. And here also the world's only true "greatness" may be again abundantly manifested.

How often, in our "daily round and common task," when many things are to be accomplished, or in wider life, when much of persistency and faithfulness is needed, the spirit within us is weak and vacillating; full of peevishness and fretfulness; doubtful, and easily vanquished. We all, indeed, often make high resolves; we all often begin great things,— things which, if followed to successful issue, should make us rich in true soul-wealth, perhaps redeem or save some one dear to us, possibly help the whole world,— which at any rate would build up our own poor lives. But the boast at the putting on of the armor is not the ease of him who successfully and continuously wears it, nor the glory of him who takes it off. And we all need, in the frequent ensuing weakness and despondency which comes to us after failure, such word of power and inspiration as that of Longfellow's paraphrase of ancient writ:

"Let not him that putteth his hand to the plow look backwards."

We need strength from every prophet that ever lived, from every wind of God that blows.

In one of the Books of Wordsworth's long poem, "The Excursion," the garrulous "Pastor" of the poem, seated with his visitors in the little inclosure nigh to his church, tells the varied story of the graveyard's humble occupants. Within the embrace of one of the lowly mounds at their feet reposed the dust of an enthusiast miner,— one who, through twenty years, toiled in vain on a near mountain-side, seeking hidden treasure. Never, during twice ten years, did his hand falter or his heart sink. And at last he was successful.

> " 'Conspicuous to this day
> The path remains that link'd his cottage-door
> To the mine's mouth; a long and slanting track
> Upon the rugged mountain's stony side,
> Worn by his daily visits to and from
> The darksome centre of a constant hope.
> That path, the force of beating wind and rain,
> Nor the vicissitudes of frost and thaw,
> Shall cause to fade, till centuries pass away.
> And it is named, in memory of the event,
> The "Path of Perseverance." '

TRUE GREATNESS. 71

> "'Power from whom
> Man has his strength!' exclaimed the Wanderer,
> 'To all the virtuous among mankind
> Be granted the keen eye which can perceive
> In this blind world the guiding vein of hope,
> That, like this laborer, such may dig their way,
> Unshaken, unseduced, unterrified.'"

Surely we may echo the Wanderer's aspiration! For in such tireless hope and persistence as this there shall always be "greatness," whether the "end sought" comes at last, or forever mocks. In untiring persistence, noble endeavor, there lies, always, more than in the gaining of what we seek. The greatest works of good in the world have ever been performed, not so much by mere "smartness," nor so much even by native ability alone, as by the persistence which urges on whatever of ability may be possessed, great or small, to some fine consummation. Samuel Johnson was fond of pointing to any high palace or stately cathedral-tower, and saying, "It was raised by single stones." And each stone raised gave *new power* to the raiser. The reward was in the faithful doing, not in the magnificence of the finished structure.

> "But the night-wind cries: 'Despair!
> Those who walk with feet of air
> Leave no long-enduring marks;
> At God's forges incandescent
> Mighty hammers beat incessant,
> Men are but the flying sparks.'
>
> "And I answer,—'Though it be,
> Why should that discomfort me?
> No endeavor is in vain;
> Its reward is in the doing,
> And the rapture of pursuing
> Is the prize the vanquished gain.'"

Happy, those who strive, yet not feverishly; who strive, yet not with pain at vanquishment, so high the seeking! And happy, those who *do*, and yet are unselfish; who do, however humbly, nor ever in their doing injure another! In all our struggle for place and success, for ampler means, and for new attainment,— in our struggle even for the doing of good to our fellows,— I deem that the prayer of poor Queen Caroline Matilda, of Denmark, which she wrote on the window of her chapel, might well be added even to our highest endeavors, as the frequent aspiration of us all: "Oh! keep me innocent! make others great!"

In a hundred departments of life I might point out the duty and necessity of "overcoming,"— with the consequent greatness of life which should ensue. We all have much to overcome in the way of selfishness. Generosity is greatness. "What shall we have!" asked the disciples, in old time, of their leader. "What shall we have, inasmuch as we have left all and followed thee?" The question is still asked, to-day; but by many who have never left anything. Indeed, "What shall I have? How much can I get? What good thing can I grasp and keep? Never mind my brother or my sister in the great world-family, but my ease and my pleasure and my storehouse and barn!"— these seem the great cry we are always hearing, high above the loudest song that all the pity and charity and fraternal love of the world, put together, can echo forth.

Our souls are sick with the world's selfishness. "Wee Sir Gibbie," in MacDonald's story,— the outcast child,— could not find and eat a crust without sharing it. When afterwards he came into wealth, the same spirit continued. The need of his fellows was his only thought. How like to that man of far years and lands, who cried: "Never will I accept private individual good!" Gautama of India! "Never will I accept private individual good. Never will I enter into blessedness alone!"

At the battle of Bannockburn (history tells us), Douglas saw Randolph, his rival, outnumbered and apparently overpowered by the enemy. He prepared to hasten to his assistance; but, seeing that Randolph was already driving them back, he cried out, "Hold, and halt! We are too late to aid them; let us not lessen the victory they have won by affecting to claim a share in it." Such examples as these retrieve our faith somewhat in mankind.

And truly, it is not what we can get, but what we can give, that in this world makes us "great." It is not what we hold all to ourselves, like little Jack Horner of the nursery-tale, in the corner with his Christmas-pie; but it is what we share, it is the good we do; it is generosity, it is the *overcoming* of selfishness, that counts in our character. "He that would be first among you, let him be servant of all."

In the multitude of further illustrations of my topic which occur to me, I would speak briefly, in the next place, of the greatness which always inheres in the power (possessed at present in the world by few) of overcoming the tendency in our human nature which impels us, always, to simple, thoughtless conformity to the ideas of others, good or bad. There is "greatness" in the power to discriminate, and greatness in the power to hold to the true, when discriminated,— whatever the opposition. If we are right, why should we care what others say of us or think of us? Is not one with the Truth "a majority" still, as in times of old? Let me use here a sentence or two of Frederick Robertson's: "This," says he, "is self-reliance,— to repose calmly on the thought which is deepest in our bosom, and be unmoved if the world will not accept it yet. To live on your own convictions against the world is to overcome the world. To believe that what is truest in you is true for all; to abide by that, certain that, while you stand firm, the world will come round to you,— that is independence. It is not difficult to get away into retirement, and there live upon your own convictions; nor is it difficult to mix with men, and follow their convictions. But to enter into the world, and there live firmly according to your conscience,— that is greatness."

Especially for all who are forward-lookers in religion,— no matter how often the temptation comes,— there should never be anxiety that the nobler faith, anywhere, should sacrifice one whit of reason, of logic, or of the scientific spirit, simply for the sake of "conformity" to the views of others, or for the sake of "the appearance of things." Indeed, unreasoning conformity, and the doing of things merely for appearance' sake, are two of the main things that men should, I deem, valiantly contend against, and always contend against. If in our truth we cannot be true; if in our religion we cannot be religious,— I believe we would better not be at all. We are pointed to greatness. Let us at least struggle thitherward.

The second of the two high tokens of greatness of which I have intended especially to speak is *the struggle for culture* — soul-culture.

I have said that the power to overcome,— to overcome evil, sin, indolence, the selfishness in us, the spirit of conformity,— is token of greatness. So also, surely, and in no less degree, is the struggle for true culture greatness. And for this reason: it is the true measure of us, as men and women,— the true measure of us, *taken by ourselves.*

Browning has suggested that that only is important in human endeavor which tends to the development of a soul. Culture is such development as this. Moreover, we saw, in the beginning of our thought, that in truth many of the lives which the world has called "great" were not really great. For they were lives seeking merely to accomplish. And no life whose main purpose is simply to accomplish can be, in the best sense, a great life. The rather, Goethe's great idea is the only true idea. As some have had the keenness to see, all through the noted autobiography of this great-minded writer the thought is prominent that a man exists not for what he can accomplish, but for what can be accomplished *in* him. We exist, that is to say, for growth in our inner being — for culture.

Men too often miss the best that is in

them. Swift said, years ago, "It is in men as in soils, where sometimes there is a vein of gold which the owner knows not of." Let me spend a moment with this thought; for, to my mind, the one great vein of gold, inclusive of all others, in every human soul, is one of which few indeed seem vividly aware.

I refer to each soul's connection with the Divine; with the High, the Noble, the Pure in the universe — the Spirit of all exalting things in the Cosmos; and the soul's consequent possibilities, within itself, of exaltation. The soul is so made!

Out of the divine the soul came; part and parcel of the divine it continues; — and shall so continue, we dream, somehow, forevermore. "I and my Father are one," — we and the Power for Good in Nature are one, — are intimately and vitally conjoined. And when man shall once begin, as a whole, to realize his greatness, — his greatness as an infinite soul, a fragment of the All-soul, — then shall he begin vividly to see the littleness and meanness with which too often he is content. Then will he begin, too, to stride upward; then will he begin to be really "great."

In the present time, as men in general live, "the unwritten and indeed unknown realities of our being put to shame all that is written and known." The most precious part of men's lives is unrecognized, uncared for,— wasted; "like an unstopped vase of effervescent and perishing ointment, exhaling unconsciously, throwing off into the absolute and eternal void the very best portions of itself." Men do not know and feel that they are of the divine. Hampered and biased in all ages by the struggle for existence; and in modern years led by an imperfect understanding of the true drift of current evolutionary thought,— or misled by a too extreme following out of one characteristic of that thought,— many have come too much to look upon themselves as, after some fashion, detached "atoms" in the universe,— differentiated; "individual." But this is to be a "fragment" only, and forever a fragment. It is never "wholeness." And it leads to selfishness. What wonder that, under this thought, in our wilfulness and blindness, we stumble often, and fall? We hold our heads high in our puny egoism. We say broadly,—*I*. "I think," "I want," "I do." And verily, within bounds, this is right and justifiable. It has its meaning.

"Nothing, not God, is greater to one than one's self is,
And I say to any man or woman, Let your soul stand cool and composed before a million universes."

But our individuality is, nevertheless, not "absolute"— it is a part of the All. We are indeed in some sense individuals, yet are we swallowed up, embraced, in a deeper Oneness — in the Infinite and Eternal Whole. Thus are all men brothers, and all indeed "children" of the one Eternal Power. There is no room for selfishness.

The distinction between the Me and the Not-me is indeed "the unsolved problem of philosophy"; yet could we, I feel, once see things as they really are,— know our true relationship with the "Not-me," the Infinite Divine,— in reverence and wonder and awe every one of us would bow the head and the heart,— and be thenceforth at peace, forever. We should say, then,— no more as we do now, with the seeming absolute emphasis, "*I* want, *I* think, *I* do"; nor would "selfishness" longer reign in our human midst. But, even with the daring of direct address to the Universe-Life, we should cry:

> "I cannot say *I* think;
> I only stand upon the thought-well's brink.
> From darkness to the sun the water bubbles up —
> *I lift it* in my cup.
> Thou only thinkest — I am thought!
> Me and my thought Thou thinkest.
> Thou art the Only One, the All-in-all,
> Yet when my soul on Thee doth call,
> And Thou dost answer out of everywhere,
> I in thy Allness have my perfect share."

He only, thus, is truly great — let me **say** again — who recognizes himself not as isolated and alone in the universe of beauty and might; but a portion of that beauty, a fragment of that might; first, last, and ever, part and parcel of the Divine; — to whom, consequently, all selfishness, all self-pandering, and all spiritual ugliness, is horror of darkness — the absence of "heaven" — a present "hell."

And *then*, in "culture" — in the exaltation of his heart and mind and soul — through Science, through Bibles, through Art, through daily work, through all the high refinements of modern life; in the seeing of Beauty and the loving of Love; in the upwelling of his affections, in the noble sharing with his fellows of all good, and in his faith in the Eternal Progress, he finds *Rest;* bowing his head, ever, upon his pillow at night, or on the lap of earth, — wherever he may be, — like a simple child upon its mother's breast; possibly with never a spoken word, or perchance only with a child's sigh of trust. But at any rate, he is at peace. His dependence is the upholding Power of the worlds, however unfathomed, with which he feels himself vitally joined. He is "lost" in that. And in his "loss" he becomes great. He no longer seeks, in anything, to be "first,"— in the spirit, that is, of any narrow self-love, or of any "rivalry" with earth-fellows. The rather, he is willingly and rejoicingly "servant of all"— of all in God's wide universe that is sweet and pure and good. Becomes great,— not, it is true, in spoils and show; in earthly conquest or earthly wealth: the Fredericks and Napoleons of the world, together with all thought of them, sink into insignificance. But great in love, joy, peace, long-suffering, gentleness, goodness, faithfulness, meekness, temperance;— to be great in which is Eternal Life *now:* eternal life open to all: the eternal life which shows us to ourselves in our true light as evermore one with the Everlasting Light; evermore "in love" with the Infinite Love, and so evermore in the enfolding Good that neither life nor death can ever mar.

OUR OTHER SELVES.

Amid the ceaseless loss and change
Of time and friends and all below —
(O things we love! how swift ye go!
O things that are! how new and strange!) —
Ah, whither shall our spirits range
A more Eternal life to know!

In Syria, Ind or Egypt sought,
One answer only have the years
Sent down to banish doubts and fears: —
Within Thyself must Heaven be caught
And captive held, — or all is tears!
For this saints died and martyrs fought.

Thyself within! Thyself within!
O friend! find here thy strength, thy peace.
Pray not that loss and change may cease, —
Pray, rather, higher heights to win!
Thy spirit's Godward wings release,
And soar thee where thou art akin!

OUR OTHER SELVES.

In every man's heart there is a dream. And the dream is a seed, nestling in quietude, waiting growth; waiting time of flower and fruit.

Strange seed! For, by and by, the man finds — towards flower-time, fruit-time — that the seed, all unbeknown, was himself; his embryo self; and what he before thought was himself was not really himself, but only the garment of himself, the husk of the seed. The *dream* was his real self. That dream he has now become; and what dreamed the dream — that which he once thought was he — is dead and forever gone. The dreamer-self was in one sense himself; but it was a fading, a passing self. There was another self, waiting for him to come up with it,— his Dream! It was that "other" self which was his real self. Ah, and thank God and man if, when finally he finds himself,— when he "comes to himself,"— he discovers himself worth finding. For there are high dreams and low dreams; holy and ignoble dreams: yet the dream in either case is himself to be, and out from what he was, like the chambered nautilus from his last-year's cell, he goes to the new self, which for himself he has created. High or low, the fruitage of his seed is himself. "As he thinketh in his heart, so is he"! As he dreamed, so he became.

Our "other selves"— those selves to which we go forward! It is these that I am to consider. For we have, all of us, two selves. And our "other" selves are well worth giving thought to. Were our dream evil; were it unkindness; were it mere bodily pandering;— or were it intellectual or moral or religious untruth,— were our dream any of these things of baseness or falsehood, and we knew we ourselves were to become our dream, then certainly it would be worth our while to ponder it,— that we might escape from it. No less worth while, be our dream noble.

Is the dream which is ours a "high" dream? These "selves" which we now are — these selves which we *call* ourselves — may not be very high; we may often be discouraged and disgusted with ourselves as we call ourselves. But our dream, I take it for granted, is high. We see nobler things! And not as we are are we; but as we dream we really are. As we would be, as we aspire to be, are we. It is our other selves, I say again, that are our real selves. This gives us courage. When we wake up by and by from this earthly sleep, we shall, I can but feel, find that what I have been saying is true. And it will be a glorious awakening! So long ago as the times of Saint Bernard, he could feel and say, "In thy book, O Lord, are written all who do what they can, though they cannot do what they would."

Let us bear within us *bright* dreams:

"The glorious end shall justify it all!"

Shall we now, through a few illustrations, try to see if, as a rule, it is not what our "dream" is that we do actually tend to become? if our other, future, and better selves are not really more our actual selves than our present, dreaming selves?

Look, first, at our boys and girls,— yours and mine. What is the great thought ever uppermost in their hearts? *"When I am a man,"*—"When I am a woman, then——!" When once they have begun to think; to say "I am I"; when once through their brain, or into their heart, has flashed a first "dream," forever thence they are no more children merely,— they live as grown-up men, as grown-up women. The ball, the hoop, the go-cart, the skipping-rope, the ride bare-back on old Dobbin, may not be discarded. But their thoughts are no longer altogether of these. Their thoughts have begun to wander through eternity. And what is that sudden sally, some day, in the upper hall; in the improvised tent on the lawn or in the back yard; or in the garret of a rainy afternoon? Clad now, even outwardly, in the bonnets and shawls, in the long coats and tall hats of their elders, Sue and Mary, Jack and Tom and Theo are bearing men's and women's parts in the world. It is not mere meaningless play. Far from it. It is the outward expression of a *deep longing* within. It is painfully in earnest.

And sometimes very practical and literal meaning it has; not alone a figurative or spiritual significance. Forty-five years ago, or more, Edwin Booth, then a mere boy, decked out in the stage-trappings of his distinguished father, trod the boards of a Baltimore boarding-house cellar, improvised into a theatre, setting forth "Richard the Third" to admiring audiences at an admission-fee of three cents. Did that mean nothing? Across the water, Hans Christian Andersen forecast, as a child, the Hans Christian Andersen to be, in the way of kobold-games, gnome-dances, and fairy-operas.

All boys and girls early have their "dream"— of some kind, in some shape. And into their dream they begin to grow! Happy if the dream be a bright, a pure one: it makes or mars their future.

Let us look at one or two others of the boys of the Past. With his leather sling and a few smooth stones from the brook, David, watching his sheep as a boy, made preparatory conquest of Goliath; with his harp lonelily beneath some olive-tree he struck the chords which by and by should entrance Saul and draw the hearts of a myriad loyal subjects. How and where, think you, into his blood — into the fibre of his brain — came David the revengeful and lustful? Did he, as a boy, dream that David too? O child! O youth! be wise in time! There are dreams that are heaven; there are dreams that are hell. Sad that, all about us, open to our vision daily, are a myriad of the young,— often hardly more than children,— dreaming dreams of manhood's saddest consciousness, yet fancying them dreams divine!

As a child amid Galilean hills, or earnest as a boy with the "doctors" of the temple, the growing Jesus dreamed ahead, and could not understand that his parents still should seek for him, and treat him as young. "Wist ye not that I must be about my Father's business?" Spirit knows nothing of time. Soul knows not age. The present had sunk for him out of sight. It was only the future — the unreal — that was real for him.

As a lad, our sweetest of all foreign bards, the thinker-poet Tennyson, dreamed his dream. When, fifty-five or sixty years ago, his first thin books of verse went out, they fared hard at hands both of critics and public. But *he* knew what they did not. He knew that that Tennyson, of the first early Lyrics, was not the real Tennyson. The real Tennyson was waiting for him beyond — waiting for him to come up with him. The real Tennyson had better things in him than those of Claribel and Isabel, Mermaids and Owls. For fourteen years he smiled all silently to himself — and worked; bringing out to beauty and to helpfulness the Tennyson that waited being. Then, "In Memoriam" sang for sorrowing hearts, yes, and for thought-weary minds no less, the Song of Peace and Trust, and showed us *Tennyson;* and the world sped on.

Milton, as a boy, dreamed of Milton as a man the writer of an Epic poem which should be a world-poem. And he said to himself, while yet a boy, "The real Milton, then, is — must be — himself, in his life, an Epic poem." And the real Milton, the later Milton, like the earlier one, *was* an Epic poem. He lived the life; the man became the dream. The dream was the man in embryo; the man was the dream in actuality.

I might cite cases opposite to these — of Neros, Borgias, Byrons, Pipers, Pomeroys. What were *their* dreams? Thought shrinks from the dissection. And even as it is, our meditation here doth give us pause.

What are we? As souls, what are we? How much of that which is "proclivity" in us, whether good or ill,— how much of that, our self which is to be, or high or low,— is born in us out of the crudeness — and the beauty — of Nature? How much of it is our inheritance from immediate ancestry? And for how much are we ourselves responsible? I cannot stay with these questions now. They press on us, and I mention them to show that I do not fail to have them in mind. But my primary purpose in this address I would not be led away from. Whatever the "birth," the "origin" of our dreams, of our "proclivities,"— whether from Chaos and old Night, or direct from God to try men's souls and make them worthy of divine possibilities,— these dreams, tendencies, proclivities, call them what we will, are present facts, and are to be guided, quelled, controlled, aggrandized, as the high ideal of man and the divine may call. That we "grow into them," and become them, whichever they be that we harbor, is the important thing for us to bear in mind: for, to a greater extent — a much greater extent than most men and women, I think, practically hold and demonstrate, we *can* guide, quell, control, or aggrandize; — and, by the noble dream, the lofty vision, show ourselves progeny of the higher in Nature; yea, show ourselves "sons of God," "heirs of God," "made a little lower than God, and crowned with glory and honor." We can do this — or we can let it go undone, and drift!

Comes Wordsworth to us, saying:

"Our birth is but a sleep, and a forgetting:
  The soul that rises with us, our life's star,
Hath elsewhere had its setting,
  And cometh from afar;
    Not in entire forgetfulness,
    And not in utter nakedness,
But trailing clouds of glory do we come,
  From God, who is our home.
Heaven lies about us in our infancy!

> Shades of the prison-house begin to close
>   Upon the growing boy,
> But he beholds the light, and whence it flows,
>   He sees in it his joy;
> The youth, who daily farther from the east
> Must travel, still is Nature's priest,
>   And by the vision splendid
>   Is on his way attended."

As little ones, heaven is close-pressing on us. For the growing boy and girl, the infinite glow (Wordsworth thinks) comes to be somewhat dimmed. The youth still retains somewhat, but only somewhat, of the brightness. And, in sorrow the poet concludes,

> "At length the man perceives it die away,
>   And fade into the light of common day."

It does. True, it does, for very many. But, oh, it need not! The glow, the roseate hues, in which all things of life and earth lie in our early childhood, need never fade. Childhood knows no doubts, no fears. All things to it are wonderful, beautiful. All things call onward! And this dear vision may continue!

Nature — God — should not grow less to us, I am sure, as we grow; but ever more, — if only our hearts were free and transparent!

> "Behold the child among his new-born blisses,
> A six-years' darling of a pigmy size!
> See, where 'mid work of his own hand he lies,
> Fretted by sallies of his mother's kisses,
> With light upon him from his father's eyes!
> See, at his feet some little plan or chart,
> Some fragment of *his dream of human life*,
> Shaped by himself with newly-learnèd art;
> And this hath now his heart,
> And unto this he frames his song."

See to it, O mothers, fathers, teachers, — see to it that the song dies not down! See that discouragements, and the constant iteration of the "hardnesses" and "bitternesses" of life, on which too often the changes are rung for childish ears, meet them not, too early! Keep the beauty of outward Nature, the order of the starry paths, ever present to their sight. Keep the sunlight of purity — inward as well as outward cleanliness — shining constant for them. Keep the glow, the brightness, of the "heaven" of their infancy of confidence and trust still about them. Keep the God-Spirit, the Soul in Nature, open to their vision — if you can show them rationally that God-Spirit. (If you cannot show them God rationally — reasonably — far better that you should shut your lips and padlock them.)

And when youth comes, let it be still the same. Let Beauty still call, — no color vanished, no sun or star paled. Let Nature still be wonderful, and the Spirit-Power, the universe's Mystic Presence, helper still. For, youth-time, doubly, trebly, is Dream-time. The "other self," which by and by shall be the real self, is being created now how forcefully!

> "How beautiful is youth! how bright it gleams
> With its illusions, aspirations, dreams!
> Book of Beginnings, Story without End,
> Each maid a heroine, and each man a friend!
> Aladdin's lamp, and Fortunatus' purse,
> That holds the treasures of the universe!
> All possibilities are in its hands,
> No danger daunts it and no foe withstands;
> In its sublime audacity of faith,
> 'Be thou removed!' it to the mountain saith,

> And with ambitious feet, secure and proud,
> Ascends the ladder leaning on the cloud!"

Youth-time! O youth-time!

> "Ah, that thou couldst know thy joy,
> Ere it passes, barefoot boy!"

And thy joy not only, but thy opportunity as well; and that thou couldst learn of will-power, and self-control, and world-sacrifice, in ways of life-blessing and life-enlarging!

There is more to-day, true, to hold the young man and woman back — but there is also more to-day to help and urge the young man and woman on — than ever before in mankind's history. Moreover, led by modern science, we rejoice to think and to believe that, for all human life, existence will be easier by and by. The things retarding will be fewer; the things on-leading will be better understood, and thus be better grasped and utilized. We live in a transition-period now, when all things, it is seen, *may* be easier. And the human race rarely sees anything good in the distance, that

that distant good is not worked up towards, and, sometime, gained. In this instance of mankind, as in the individual instance, humanity's other and better self is *itself to be*. It dreams, and it becomes its dream. Our children's children, and theirs to follow, shall be of purer strain of blood, of firmer will, of clearer sight, of loftier purpose, than were our fathers, or than we are. Let us all help the easier time on, by leading the feet of our youth and maidens *now* in the Paths of Flowers; by kindling in their hearts the "dream" of the earthly Blessedness in store, causing them to believe in it, and to so run that they may, at least in part, attain to the better things than we. Let us teach them,— out of the Great Book of Nature, which, as I say, is more and more, in wise ways, being opened to us now in these our prophetic years, our splendid To-day,— teach them, show them, that Order and Beauty are the Way of Life; that he who would be blest in his daily walk, and at last reach any heaven worth having, must in his daily walk seek simplicity, and independence, and good; must think for himself, decide for himself, act for himself (of course first making himself competent); must abjure all evil and every show of evil, whether in mind or heart or life, in business or politics or religion; grasping as the soul's sure stay and lure the Good in Nature, the Better Good to be, and the fact that on man and man's faithfulness — not on miracle, nor on the supernatural, nor on sacrifices vicarious, but *on man and man's faithfulness*, the realizing of the Better Good depends. For Mankind, no less than for individual men, we must say, As its dream is, so shall be its endeavor; as its "other self" is, so shall it find its true self to be; as its dream, so shall it become.

What is it that, after nineteen centuries of the popular Christian preaching, keeps man, in his ordinary religious thought, still so low? Is it not because the religious "dreams" of the "fathers" were in reality theological and speculative "nightmares" largely, rather than open, natural vision? nightmares born of ignorance and fear — fear of Nature and dread of the future — till at last the horror of ghosts and devils, and the dream-torture of hells deepening into hells, came to be worked into the blood and brain-fibre of the race? coming into fearful and saddening consciousness of themselves in Augustine and Dante and Milton and Calvin and Edwards, and still marring and distorting even the higher and truer vision of our nobler age? Thank heaven, and the growing human science and love of our time, however, the world is at last slowly waking from its horrid sleep! Our children, if we are faithful, shall have dreams of life and its meaning, of the universe and its immanent Spirit-Presence, and of man's relation to the universe, truer, and therefore lovelier and sweeter.

I have spoken, thus far, largely of the young. But all who are of greater growth — children of Nature still, and of the God-power, though in middle life or older — need also the help and inspiration of the thought here.

The young not alone dream; the middle-aged dream too, — for good, for ill. Aaron Burr dreamed, — of British gold and British office. His dream was selfishness, and he became his dream. His shunned and bitter end we would not emulate for all the gold of the British Isles. Daniel Webster dreamed — at first, and for long, now nobly! but again, in some fateful moment — alas! was it lurking self again, in other guise, but not less fateful? Emerson dreamed, — it was of transcendent good; it was vision of man's market-cart harnessed to the chariot of the sun. Our Samuel Longfellow dreamed — his dream was never marred. It was of faith in good, of religion free yet faultless. Both men met rebuke. From a world not ready for ideal honesty, not ready for religion free, both men felt at some time the sting of neglect. But both grew grandly to their dream's bold height,— and growing, drew the world to them in love. In lesser ways, so may we all.

And the "judgment" for us — in the eye of man's progress and humanity's gain, if not in the eye of the shortseeing world — is not alone what we accomplish, but what we fain *would* accomplish. Not wholly what victory we reach, but the high thing we seek. The dream alone counts, not the failure to reach it, — if it be dream of good.

> "What I aspired to be,
> And was not, comforts me."

> "All instincts immature,
> All purposes unsure,
> All I could never be,
> All men ignored in me —
> That I am worth to God!"

No man can dream the dream of good, strive for high victory, for the universal welfare, and wholly fail. Within himself at least, he grows,— and this is the growth that counts. "When a man says, 'Virtue, I am thine; thee will I serve, day and night, in great and in small,' then is the end of Creation answered, and God is well pleased." Moreover, for such a man or woman, petty things in life, and things high, soon begin to assume their proper and comparative place. Well is it said, If the life be devoted to great dreams, great ends, minor things, of an annoying nature, will cease to irritate. One who is dreaming noble dreams, who is busy with plans which call for his best efforts, has no time to give to trivial occurrences, which are unpleasant, and which grow by undue attention. The rather, with our Woodsman Poet, he grows to say and feel — to consciously realize —

"I seem ensphered within a glory-zone
Of heavenly beauty — and it is *my own!*
Where'er I go, it goes; and night or day
It is the same, forever and alway.
From good intent the rays of glory flow,
And light the path where'er my feet may go.

"The eternal verities, from where I stand,
  Loom up like mountains, beautiful and grand.
 Henceforth I fear not, for I plainly see
 All things are safe, and shall forever be.
  I cease my quest — the short days fly
   On wings of morn or even;
  Yet more and more the universe grows I,
   And I myself am heaven."

We have, however, our choice. Our dream is our own, — it depends on ourselves. "The gods implore not, plead not, solicit not: they only offer choice and occasion." Do we let choice and occasion go by? They go by! Do we choose the lower? The choice is made! But in the lower is no "satisfaction." The selection of things "eternal" — things permanent in the economy of the Cosmos — this alone is what marks us "of God," of the Lofty One, of the High and Holy One that inhabiteth eternity.

Treasures of purity! of the spirit of truth-loving, of the spirit of progress, — of love, joy, peace, long-suffering, gentleness, goodness, faithfulness, meekness, temperance! — yea, make we these our dream. And lay them up — within! in God's innermost temple of the soul — where neither moth nor rust can corrupt, nor thieves break through to steal. Then come unto your own, — and your own shall receive you!

Virtue, — the on-leading good, — the intangible yet mighty good, — the "spiritual," — is forever and alone the victorious and permanent; is "that which endures and is, while the material, which seems to be, is but fleeting, and perishes." What else, then, shall we make our dream? What else shall we depend on? This is the only actual *worth* dreaming, worth coming into; is, by Nature's grace, our real other self! And, dreaming that, and seeing its Beauty, we can grow into nothing better in all God's universe.

Happy for us if we learn, while yet there is time, that earth's "material" things, the trifles even of our daily lives, — its burdens, its envies, its stings, — may all be transmuted, transfigured, into the spiritual; that the "perishable" may be stamped with imperishable worth. Then we are on the road to Eternal Good; we know the Present Heaven, not wait alone for an Abode of Bliss in the Future. Nor shall we fail to be helping to draw others along with us also, in our train.

We shall not fail, either, of finally finding our "other self" worth merging our present self into! We shall find our other selves to be of the divine, and shall be at last able to say,— with our own interpretation of that phrase,— "I and my Father are one." We shall *be* the Love we have loved.

"I shall be satisfied when I awake in thy likeness."

"Excellent books, of high purpose."—*Minneapolis Journal.*

WRITINGS BY JAMES H. WEST.

IN LOVE WITH LOVE. Four Life-Studies. Cloth, bevelled, red edges, 109 pages, 50 cents.

CONTENTS: Transfigurations; Serenity; True Greatness; Our Other Selves.

THE COMPLETE LIFE. Six Addresses. Cloth, 112 pages, 50 cents.

"Words brave and true. Every word the author indites is golden, and should be read by young and old. Such books are genuine uplifts of heart and mind, and when we get to heaven, if we ever do, through earth's sordid dust and mire, we shall have men like James H. West to thank for finding our way there."—*Chicago Evening Journal.*

UPLIFTS OF HEART AND WILL. In Prose and Verse. *Second Thousand, with additions.* Cloth, bevelled, red edges, 106 pages, 50 cents.

"It is a good sign that Mr. West's little book has sold so well. They have been to many just what they are called—uplifts of heart and will."—*Christian Register.*

"It is a book to aid and inspire by its expressions of lofty truth and noble aspirations in prose and poetry."—*Public Opinion.*

HOLIDAY IDLESSE, and Other Poems. New Red-Line Edition. Illustrated. Cloth, 252 pages, $1.00.

"His poems rank easily in the higher grade of those published in these days."—*Congregationalist.*

"Excellent verse, of a very genuine sort,—full of poetic suggestiveness, aspiration and the glow of true feeling.... Unusually clear in outline and strong in expression."—*Christian Union.*

SONGS OF SINCERITY. (*Compilation.*) Heavy paper, card covers, 10 cents.

A collection of seventy-five pieces, progressive in idea and lofty in hope, certain of them never before collected, by such authors as Samuel Longfellow, John W. Chadwick, F. L. Hosmer, and others; and it includes, also, words by Emerson, Lowell, Whittier, H. W. Longfellow, Wm. C. Gannett, M. J. Savage, Clough, Wasson, Matthew Arnold, Jones Very, Alice Cary, Lucy Larcom, Harriet Prescott Spofford, Mrs. Hemans, the compiler, and others.

[SECOND THOUSAND.]

UPLIFTS OF HEART AND WILL.

In Prose and Verse.

By JAMES H. WEST,

Author of "The Complete Life," "In Love with Love," etc.

"It takes a soul to move a body.
* * Life develops from within."

PRESS NOTICES:

London Inquirer.— Helpful and interesting. The fact that a second thousand has been called for will be some guarantee of such a book's claim to notice.

Sacramento Record-Union.— One of the most earnest volumes we have ever seen; marked by an originality that renders it peculiarly attractive.

Fall River Monitor.— They touch upon the many experiences of the ordinary daily life; they have a wide comprehension of man's needs, and a still wider, deeper sympathy with his aspirations, his spiritual gains and losses.

London Christian Life.— A book good for both old and young and for all alike.

Yale Literary Magazine.— The poems included in the book are impressive, many of them being of a high order.

Woman's Tribune.— Not dogmatic, deeply reverent, appealing to the divine within the human soul, calling it to the heights of larger helpfulness and blessedness.

Cleveland World.— A beautiful little volume, free from cant, and full of love, truth and broad humanitarianism.

American Hebrew.— Prose and verse that will surely appeal to an ever-widening circle of readers. It is gratifying to know that a new edition has been demanded.

London Christian World.— Full of very helpful and finely uttered things. The poems have in them a thrill of intense reality.

Boston Herald.— One is very strongly impressed with the sincerity and reality of expression.

The Unitarian.— The earnestness, indeed the eagerness, of the writer cannot fail to quicken a helpful and elevating aspiration in the heart of every reader.

Cloth, bevelled, red edges, 106 pages, 50 cents.

** *For sale by booksellers, or sent postpaid on receipt of price.*

Books of Interest and Value.

Character and Love.

Compiled and arranged by ALFRED W. MARTIN, from the Religious and Moral Writings of all lands and times. Cloth, 50 cents.

Topics: Brotherhood, True Worship, Character, Holy Living, Selflessness, Diligence, Integrity, Duty, Loyalty to Truth, God, Tolerance, Manhood, Nature, Justice, Humility, Obedience, Life, Fraternity of Religions, Prophets and Sages, Prayer, The Commonwealth of Man, and others.

Proofs of Evolution.

The evidences from Geology, Morphology, Embryology, Metamorphosis, Rudimentary Organs, Geographical Distribution, Discovered Links, Artificial Breeding, Reversion, Mimicry. By NELSON C. PARSHALL. Cloth, 70 pages, 50 cents.

"One of the most systematic, concise and comprehensive presentations in popular form of the foundation and theory of evolution. Excellent, . . . succinct, . . . interesting."—*Public Opinion.*

The New Ideal.

A volume of original popular essays and reviews,—Modern Religious, Scientific, Economic, Reformatory. Edited by JAMES H. WEST. Cloth, 570 pages, $1.50.

"Of marked ability. Indispensable to those who seek to keep abreast of contemporary thought."—*Springfield Times.*

"Deserving of attention from thoughtful persons."—*Boston Herald.*

Freedom and Fellowship in Religion.

Essays on Vital Topics of Ethics and Religion. By O. B. FROTHINGHAM, J. W. CHADWICK, Col. T. W. HIGGINSON, W. J. POTTER, SAMUEL LONGFELLOW, F. E. ABBOT, Ph.D., and others. 424 pages, $1.00.

Some of the Topics: Religion and Science; The Religious Outlook; Liberty and the Church; The Nature of Religion; Philanthropy; The Soul of Protestantism; The Genius of Christianity.

Two Books of Large Value.

Evolution. *The Origin of Things.*

Fifteen Popular Lectures on Important Modern Themes, by John W. Chadwick, M. J. Savage, Dr. Lewis G. Janes, E. D. Cope, Ph.D., and others. Cloth, 408 pages, $2.00.

CONTENTS:

Life of Herbert Spencer; Life of Darwin; How Suns and Planets Grew; Evolution of the Earth; Vegetal Evolution; Evolution of Animal Life; The Descent of Man; Evolution of Mind; Evolution of Society; Evolution of Theology; Evolution of Morals; Proofs of Evolution; Evolution as related to Religious Thought; The Philosophy of Evolution; The Effects of Evolution on the Coming Civilization.

"Scholarly and instructive. We commend the book "—*New York Sun.*

"A simple but accurate exposition of the evolutionary philosophy."—*Science (New York).*

Sociology. *The Growth of Man.*

Seventeen Popular Lectures on Important Modern Themes, by Prof. John Fiske, John W. Chadwick, Dr. Lewis G. Janes, John C. Kimball, and others. Cloth, 412 pages, $2.00.

CONTENTS:

The Scope and Principles of the Evolution Philosophy; The Relativity of Knowledge; Primitive Man; Growth of the Marriage Relation; Evolution of the State; Evolution of Law; Evolution of Medical Science; Evolution of Arms and Armor; Evolution of the Mechanic Arts; Evolution of the Wages System; Education as a Factor in Civilization; The Theological Method in Social Reform; The Socialistic Method in Social Reform; The Anarchistic Method in Social Reform; The Scientific Method in Social Reform; Life of Asa Gray; Life of E. L. Youmans.

"A very brilliant book indeed. One can here get at the core of all the dominant isms."—*Minneapolis Journal.*

"A great educational work. There is a whole world of information in these papers."—*Brooklyn Standard-Union.*

Druck:
Customized Business Services GmbH
im Auftrag der KNV-Gruppe
Ferdinand-Jühlke-Str. 7
99095 Erfurt